D1379610

DOGS SET XI

ALASKAN MALAMUTES

Kristin Petrie
ABDO Publishing Company

visit us at
www.abdopublishing.com

Published by ABDO Publishing Company, PO Box 398166, Minneapolis, MN 55439.
Copyright © 2014 by Abdo Consulting Group, Inc. International copyrights reserved
in all countries. No part of this book may be reproduced in any form without written
permission from the publisher. The Checkerboard Library™ is a trademark and logo of
ABDO Publishing Company.

Printed in the United States of America, North Mankato, Minnesota.
102013
012014

 PRINTED ON RECYCLED PAPER

Cover Photo: Alamy
Interior Photos: Alamy pp. 5, 6, 10, 17, 21; Corbis pp. 9, 13; Glow Images p. 15;
    SuperStock pp. 7, 11, 14, 19

Editors: Rochelle Baltzer, Megan M. Gunderson
Art Direction: Neil Klinepier

Library of Congress Cataloging-in-Publication Data

Petrie, Kristin, 1970-
 Alaskan Malamutes / Kristin Petrie.
    pages cm. -- (Dogs)
 Includes index.
 ISBN 978-1-62403-100-7
1. Alaskan Malamute--Juvenile literature. I. Title.
 SF429.A67P48 2014
 636.73--dc23
                        2013025484

CONTENTS

THE DOG FAMILY

Long ago, dogs were not just for walking, cuddling, and playing. The first dogs were used for hunting. These dogs descended from another member of the family **Canidae**, the gray wolf.

Members of the family Canidae have excellent senses of sight and smell. They have strong instincts to protect themselves and to find food. Through the centuries, humans used these and other helpful canine skills to meet their needs.

Some dogs are bold and territorial, which makes them good watchdogs. Others are calm and love attention. These dogs make wonderful companions. Strength and **endurance** make for great working dogs. One working dog played a vital role in the lives of its people. This is the Alaskan malamute.

Today, the Alaskan malamute is one of more than 400 dog breeds.

ALASKAN MALAMUTES

The Alaskan malamute ranks in the AKC's top 60 most popular dogs.

The Alaskan malamute was developed in the 1800s by a native Inuit tribe known as the Mahlemuts. They settled on the Kotzebue Sound in the upper-western part of what is now Alaska. To transport food and supplies across this icy land, they needed a powerful dog.

Alaskan malamutes were the intelligent, hardworking dogs they desired. This **breed** had the **endurance** and strength to pull heavy sleds over long distances. Their thick coats protected them from

harsh weather. Malamutes also hunted for food and protected their people from polar bears!

Over time, the **breed**'s popularity grew. Malamutes were used for expeditions to the South Pole. During **World War I**, they brought supplies to French troops by sled in bad weather. Then in 1935, the breed was recognized by the **American Kennel Club (AKC)**.

The Alaskan malamute is named for the Mahlemuts. It is called the "mal" for short.

QUALITIES

Despite its large size and wolf-like appearance, the Alaskan malamute is a playful, affectionate dog. Its friendly nature extends beyond family and friends to strangers. For this reason, the Alaskan malamute does not make a good guard dog!

Instead, this gentle temperament makes the **breed** a good match for families with children. Still, all family members must know how to master the malamute's independent nature. If not kept in their place, these strong-willed dogs will attempt to run the household!

With early **socialization**, the Alaskan malamute also enjoys being with other large pets. However, the breed's strong instinct to hunt never goes away. Small pets may look like prey!

Another strong malamute instinct is digging. A bored malamute's digging can be destructive. And, digging under a fence and escaping can be dangerous.

Properly trained malamutes are intensely loyal and bonded to their families.

COAT AND COLOR

The Alaskan malamute has a heavy double coat. The coarse outer coat is short to medium in length. It increases in length around the neck and shoulders. This longer hair continues down the Alaskan malamute's back. A large plume of hair covers the **breed**'s tail.

Malamutes have thick paw pads and fur between their toes. This protects their "snowshoe" feet and lets them spend long hours on the snow.

The malamute's **dense** undercoat is one to two inches (2.5 to 5 cm) thick. Its woolly texture and natural oils keep out water and the cold. In fact,

A malamute's face is unique! Some are all white. Others are marked with a bar or a mask.

malamutes can survive at temperatures as low as -70 degrees Fahrenheit (-55°C)!

The **breed**'s heavy coat **sheds** seasonally. This leaves a shorter, lighter coat for warmer summer months.

The Alaskan malamute's underbody and feet and sections of its legs are always white. White also defines the malamute's face markings. Other markings range in color. Some malamutes have light gray to black markings. Others have brown to red markings. Still other malamutes are pure white.

SIZE

The Alaskan malamute is a majestic and powerfully built dog. Its deep chest and heavily muscled shoulders are perfect for pulling heavy loads. The malamute's strong, large-boned legs are made for hard work.

Like the rest of its body, the Alaskan malamute's head is big and impressive. It features triangular ears and brown, almond-shaped eyes. The malamute's large **muzzle** bears its strong jaw and black or brown nose.

Male Alaskan malamutes stand an impressive 25 inches (64 cm) at the shoulders. They usually weigh 85 pounds (39 kg), but they can weigh more than 100 pounds (45 kg)! Females are slightly smaller. They are 23 inches (58 cm) tall and weigh 75 pounds (34 kg).

Malamutes are one of the oldest Arctic sled dogs. Their size and build make them ideal for hauling heavy loads over long distances. They are not built for speed.

CARE

*Swimming is great exercise for some malamutes.
But, others do not like the water.*

One of the most important ways to care for
your malamute is to provide exercise and attention!
Playing, walking, and grooming are great ways to
meet these needs.

New owners must prepare for frequent brushing.
This means at least three times a week but can

mean daily! Be sure the brush or comb reaches through the dog's thick fur to its skin. This helps distribute natural oils and keep the coat and skin healthy. A few baths per year will also help.

Like all dogs, the Alaskan malamute's teeth must be cleaned regularly. Brushing with dog toothpaste leads to less bacteria, illness, bad breath, and tooth loss! Start brushing your dog's teeth as a puppy.

All dogs also need a good doctor. Veterinarians provide **vaccines** and perform checkups. They **spay** and **neuter** pets. Veterinarians can also detect elbow, hip, vision, and other problems common to this **breed**.

This intelligent breed enjoys agility training, which involves obstacle courses!

FEEDING

Dogs require a balanced diet to maintain their health and provide energy. Quality commercial dog foods come in dry, moist, and semimoist varieties.

The amount of food needed depends on several factors. These include a dog's age, activity level, and size. Puppies need several small meals of puppy food daily to support rapid growth. Large, active adult dogs need more food. Split up food into two or three meals per day. This helps prevent **bloat**.

Whatever your pet's age, watch for unhealthy weight gain. This **breed** likes to eat! If allowed, a malamute will eat all of its own food plus yours. Choose large, sturdy dog dishes to keep the malamute from chewing them. Don't worry, puppies will grow into them!

Another important part of the malamute's diet is water. Limit water during mealtime to help prevent **bloat**. But, provide plenty of fresh water the rest of the day. This is especially important during exercise and in hot weather.

If you decide to change your dog's food, do so gradually. This will help prevent stomach upset.

THINGS THEY NEED

The athletic Alaskan malamute has a great need for activity and exercise. A large, fenced yard is an ideal place for this. Otherwise long, frequent walks or time in other open spaces are essential. Malamutes without enough exercise become bored and destructive.

A sturdy collar, identification tags, and a leash are needed for those long walks. The malamute's friendly nature may have him greeting every stranger. But not everyone appreciates greetings from large dogs, especially dogs that look like wolves! So, keep your malamute close.

All dogs need a few more supplies to live comfortably. A crate provides an ideal space for rest and sleep. It is also helpful for training and travel. And don't forget a variety of safe toys!

Malamutes love spending time with their owners. Even adult rescue dogs will form strong bonds.

PUPPIES

Like other dogs, the female malamute is **pregnant** for around 63 days after mating. Newborn puppies are blind, deaf, and nearly helpless.

Approximately 10 to 14 days after birth, puppies gain their sight and sense of hearing. They soon begin wandering around and playing with one another. Their mother continues to care for and nurse them until they can eat solid foods. This starts around four weeks.

Good **breeders** keep puppies with their mother and siblings until they are eight to ten weeks old. This amount of time allows for proper **weaning** and early **socialization**.

When you decide to welcome a malamute puppy into your life, choose a healthy one. It should

have a shiny coat, clear eyes, and clean ears. It should be active, alert, and eager to meet you. A healthy, happy Alaskan malamute will be a loving companion for 10 to 14 years.

At three weeks, puppies begin exploring their world. Human handling is important at this time. Later, this will help the puppies bond with their owners.

GLOSSARY

American Kennel Club (AKC) - an organization that studies and promotes interest in purebred dogs.

bloat - a condition in which food and gas trapped in a dog's stomach cause pain, shock, and even death.

breed - a group of animals sharing the same ancestors and appearance. A breeder is a person who raises animals. Raising animals is often called breeding them.

Canidae (KAN-uh-dee) - the scientific Latin name for the dog family. Members of this family are called canids. They include wolves, jackals, foxes, coyotes, and domestic dogs.

dense - thick or compact.

endurance - the ability to sustain a long, stressful effort or activity.

muzzle - an animal's nose and jaws.

neuter (NOO-tuhr) - to remove a male animal's reproductive glands.

pregnant - having one or more babies growing within the body.

shed - to cast off hair, feathers, skin, or other coverings or parts by a natural process.

socialization - adapting an animal to behaving properly around people or other animals in various settings.

spay - to remove a female animal's reproductive organs.

vaccine (vak-SEEN) - a shot given to prevent illness or disease.

wean - to accustom an animal to eating food other than its mother's milk.

World War I - from 1914 to 1918, fought in Europe.

WEB SITES

To learn more about Alaskan malamutes, visit ABDO Publishing Company online. Web sites about Alaskan malamutes are featured on our Book Links page. These links are routinely monitored and updated to provide the most current information available.

www.abdopublishing.com

INDEX